Causes and Effects of the American Civil War

G. O'Muhr

The Rosen Publishing Group's
PowerKids Press™
New York

Published in 2009 by The Rosen Publishing Group, Inc.
29 East 21st Street, New York, NY 10010

Book Design: Michael J. Flynn

Photo Credits: Cover © Steve Estvanik/Shutterstock; pp. 3–32 (paper and wood background) © Petrov Stanislav Eduardovich/Shutterstock; pp. 5 (slaves harvesting), 7 (plantation), 18 (John Breckinridge), 21 (Fort Sumter) © Bettmann/Corbis; p. 7 (city) © Hulton-Deutsch Collection/Corbis; pp. 9 (signing of Constitution), 10 (James Madison), 14 (poster), 15 (fugitive slaves), 25 (Sherman's march) © MPI/Stringer/Hulton Archive/Getty Images; p. 11 (Constitution) © Mark R./Shutterstock; p. 13 (Henry Clay) © Stock Montage/Hulton Archive/Getty Images; p. 16 (Dred Scott) http://upload.wikimedia.org/wikipedia/commons/9/97/DredScott.jpg; p. 17 (John Brown) http://upload.wikimedia.org/wikipedia/en/0/07/John_brown_abo.jpg; p. 17 (Harpers Ferry) http://upload.wikimedia.org/wikipedia/commons/f/f1/John_brown_interior_engine_house.jpg; p. 18 (Stephen Douglas) http://upload.wikimedia.org/wikipedia/commons/a/a0/Stephen_Arnold_Douglas.jpg; p. 19 (Abraham Lincoln) http://upload.wikimedia.org/wikipedia/commons/f/fe/Abraham_Lincoln_seated%2C_Feb_9%2C_1864.jpg; p. 23 (Lincoln and generals) http://upload.wikimedia.org/wikipedia/commons/c/c3/Lincoln_and_generals_at_Antietam.jpg; p. 27 (Lincoln funeral) http://upload.wikimedia.org/wikipedia/en/9/9d/Lincoln_funeral_in_New_York_City.jpg; p. 28 (Andrew Johnson) http://upload.wikimedia.org/wikipedia/commons/2/23/Andrew_Johnson_-_3a53290u.png; p. 29 (Johnson trial) http://upload.wikimedia.org/wikipedia/commons/d/d2/Andew_Johnson_impeachment_trial.jpg.

Library of Congress Cataloging-in-Publication Data

O'Muhr, G.
  Causes and effects of the American Civil War / G. O'Muhr.
       p. cm.
  Includes index.
  ISBN: 978-1-4358-0203-2 (pbk.)
  6-pack ISBN: 978-1-4358-0204-9
  ISBN 978-1-4358-3013-4 (lib. bdg.)
  1. United States—History—Civil War, 1861-1865—Juvenile literature. I. Title.
  E468.O575 2009
  973.7'11-dc22

                                    2008047090

Contents

A Divided Nation

When most Americans hear the term "civil war," they think of the war fought within the United States during the mid-1800s. This was a terrible time for the nation. More American lives were lost during the American Civil War than during any other war in U.S. history. What caused this conflict?

Most people can name one cause—slavery. In the 1800s, slavery truly divided the nation. However, other issues led to the American Civil War as well. Another cause was disagreement about what powers and rights the states possessed and how strong the federal government should be. Government leaders had argued these issues since the establishment of the United States. The founding fathers created the U.S. Constitution and assigned certain powers to the federal government and other powers to state governments. However, they left the issue of slavery to be addressed at a later time.

By the mid-1800s, slavery couldn't be ignored. Also by that time, the Northern and Southern economies and interests had become different, which caused more arguments about how the country should be governed. Arguments led to violence, and violence became more frequent. The American Civil War soon followed, and its effects changed the nation forever.

Children born into slavery worked alongside their parents. However, they were sometimes sold and separated from their families.

Trouble in the New Nation

You've probably heard the phrase "all men are created equal." In 1776, America's founding fathers used these words in the Declaration of Independence when they formally stated that the colonies were establishing their own nation. They wanted rights and freedoms for "all men."

Slavery

Unfortunately, the founding fathers didn't really mean all men. One group they left out included about 500,000 people—slaves. Although many people were against slavery, some thought trying to bar slavery would keep the colonies from uniting. These people, including Thomas Jefferson, hoped that slavery would be banned someday, but also thought they must allow it for a time. This was a major issue at the **Constitutional Convention** of 1787.

Economic Differences Between the North and South

Differing economies in the North and South led to differing opinions about slavery. By the late 1700s, the North was a center of trade and was building an industrial economy. There were some slaves but also thousands of free blacks. The Southern states still relied on an agricultural economy. Tobacco, cotton, and sugarcane were major crops, and the huge Southern

By the mid-1800s, the Southern agricultural economy depended on slaves as a workforce (below), whereas the North focused on trade and industry (right).

7

plantations needed many laborers. Black slaves supplied this labor. Leaders in the Southern states feared that their economies would be ruined without slave labor.

State and Federal Powers

The Constitutional Convention's representatives disagreed about how to divide power between the federal and state governments. Some worried that a strong federal government would take away the rights of the individual states. The colonies had experienced unfair laws under the British government. Would a strong federal government repeat this power struggle? Many people felt more loyalty to their state and its interests than to their nation.

However, if states had more power than the federal government, could they work together as one nation? To some, it seemed as if too much state power created thirteen small nations.

Compromises at the Convention

In order to unite the colonies, the representatives at the Constitutional Convention resolved their differences through compromises. First, the writers of the Constitution included a section stating that the

George Washington (standing in black) was president of the Constitutional Convention of 1787. This painting shows the representatives at the signing of the Constitution.

federal government couldn't regulate the slave trade until 1808. That year, the issue could be addressed again.

As one way to address the division of power between the states and the federal government, the convention created a national government with three branches led by the Congress, the president, and the Supreme Court.

Congress, the lawmaking branch, would be made up of representatives from each state. In this way, the states had power over federal laws governing their citizens.

Congress was composed of two houses—the Senate and the House of Representatives. Two senators from each state sat in the Senate. The number of representatives each state sent to the House of Representatives depended on the state's population. This presented a problem for many Southern states that were largely populated by slaves. Without counting the slaves (often thought of as property rather than as people), they would have fewer representatives and less voting power. These states worried that antislavery states would gain power in Congress. A compromise was reached that counted each slave as three-fifths of a person.

James Madison, a convention representative and later U.S. president, helped work out the three-fifths section of the Constitution. Of the compromise,

James Madison

he wrote, "It seemed now to be pretty well understood that the real difference of interests lay not between the large and small but between the northern and southern states. The institution of slavery and its consequences formed the line."

Some call James Madison the "Father of the Constitution" for his contributions to the document. He later wrote the Bill of Rights.

Balancing Issues

The Constitutional Convention succeeded in creating a nation but didn't solve the issue of slavery. Decisions had to be made about whether slavery would be allowed in new states that became part of the nation. At first, the border was the **Mason-Dixon Line** and the Ohio River. As the United States expanded west of the Mississippi River and across North America, new rules were needed.

The Missouri Compromise (also called the Compromise of 1820) was an agreement in which Maine was admitted to the union as a free state and Missouri as a slave state. This maintained the balance between the number of

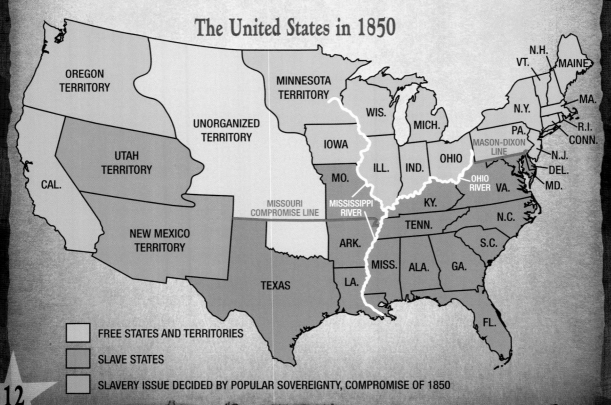

The United States in 1850

- OREGON TERRITORY
- MINNESOTA TERRITORY
- N.H.
- VT.
- MAINE
- UNORGANIZED TERRITORY
- WIS.
- N.Y.
- MA.
- PA.
- R.I.
- CONN.
- MASON-DIXON LINE
- UTAH TERRITORY
- IOWA
- MICH.
- N.J.
- OHIO
- DEL.
- ILL.
- IND.
- OHIO RIVER
- CAL.
- MO.
- VA.
- MD.
- MISSOURI COMPROMISE LINE
- MISSISSIPPI RIVER
- KY.
- NEW MEXICO TERRITORY
- TENN.
- N.C.
- ARK.
- S.C.
- TEXAS
- MISS.
- ALA.
- GA.
- LA.
- FL.

- FREE STATES AND TERRITORIES
- SLAVE STATES
- SLAVERY ISSUE DECIDED BY POPULAR SOVEREIGNTY, COMPROMISE OF 1850

free states and the number of slave states. Any future states created from the **Louisiana Territory** above a certain line of latitude would be free states. Those below would be slave states.

However, the United States gained new territory after a war with Mexico in the 1840s. The Compromise of 1850 followed. California entered the nation as a free state, and settlers in New Mexico and Utah were allowed to vote on the issue of slavery. This was called **popular sovereignty**. In addition, the Compromise of 1850 outlawed the slave trade in Washington, D.C., but allowed slavery to continue there.

Senator Henry Clay of Virginia proposed the Compromise of 1850. Congress discussed it for 8 months before finally passing it. Clay had worked on the Missouri Compromise as well.

The Fugitive Slave Act

Another part of the Compromise of 1850 was the Fugitive Slave Act. This law required people to turn in runaway slaves. It also took away a slave's right to a trial, which meant that even a free black could be accused of being an escaped slave and sent to the South.

The Fugitive Slave Act greatly angered those against slavery, called abolitionists. To them, it meant that the laws in slave states were being forced on free states. The antislavery movement grew stronger. The Underground Railroad—a combination of routes and people who guided slaves to freedom— worked even harder to succeed. Before slavery ended, the Underground Railroad had guided perhaps as many as 100,000 slaves to freedom in the northern United States and Canada.

The Kansas-Nebraska Act

In 1854, the Kansas-Nebraska Act created two new territories. The Compromise of 1850 had promised popular sovereignty to the residents of Kansas and Nebraska. However, abolitionists pointed out that the Compromise of 1820 had drawn a line

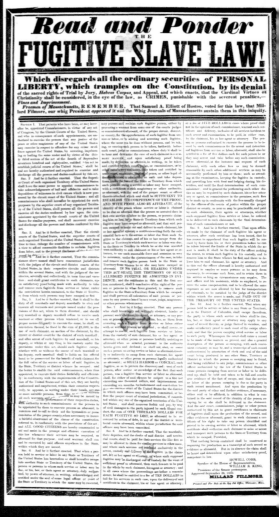

This abolitionist paper was posted in Massachusetts in 1850.

This illustration shows fear and pain on the faces of slaves as they attempt escape.

CAUSE: Some people wanted to abolish the practice of slavery, while others thought it was acceptable.

CAUSE: People argued about the powers of state governments compared to the powers of the federal government. Which should make slavery laws?

CAUSE: The North and South had different economies and therefore different interests. The South wanted slavery to supply the workforce for their agricultural economy.

EFFECT: American Civil War

of latitude between slave and free states. No state above that line could be a slave state. Both new states were above that line. Which law would stand?

President Franklin Pierce voted for popular sovereignty. As a result, people who lived outside of Kansas and Nebraska rushed in to vote. At one location, only 20 of 600 voters were state residents! The results made both Kansas and Nebraska free states. However, violence at the polls led to the nickname "Bleeding Kansas."

Dred Scott and the Supreme Court

In 1857, the U.S. Supreme Court weighed in on the slavery debate. Dred Scott, a black slave from Missouri, had lived with his owner in the free state of Illinois and the free territory of Wisconsin before moving back to Missouri. Scott went to court to gain his freedom, believing that he had become free once he had lived in those areas. However, the court ruled that blacks weren't citizens and therefore couldn't go to court. It also ruled that the federal government couldn't ban slavery in any territory and that this issue was within each state's power. This ruling was a blow to abolitionists and to those who thought the federal government should have the power to make laws regarding slavery.

Dred Scott

John Brown and Harpers Ferry

John Brown

About the same time as the Dred Scott case, a white farmer named John Brown began to encourage violence as a way to defeat slavery. He and his followers killed several slavery supporters in Kansas. He then organized a break-in at a federal **armory** in Harpers Ferry, Virginia (now West Virginia). The group took weapons and called for slaves in the South to rise up against their owners. Brown was captured and hanged. However, he became a hero to many abolitionists. A popular song was later written about him. Some wondered if Brown was correct—perhaps the slavery issue could only be settled with violence.

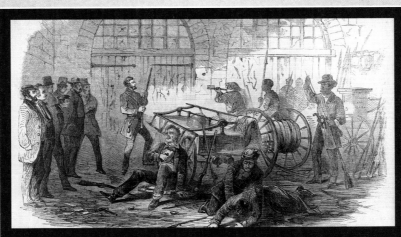

John Brown and his followers locked themselves in the armory. However, soldiers broke down the door.

17

The Election of 1860

By the presidential election of 1860, the issue of slavery had touched every part of the nation. It affected political parties as well. The Republican Party formed in 1854 and stood firmly against slavery. Many members of the other existing parties joined the Republicans.

Abraham Lincoln, a senator from Illinois, became the Republican candidate for president. Stephen Douglas ran for a party called the Northern Democrats, which was mostly against slavery. John Breckinridge was the candidate for the Southern Democratic Party, which mostly supported slavery.

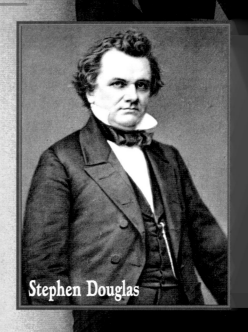

Stephen Douglas

Lincoln won the election, mainly because supporters of the Democratic Party had split their votes between the party's two candidates. Lincoln received about 40 percent of the popular vote, which was more than anyone else. In addition, he had won the most **electoral** votes. Southern states were angry at his victory, especially since Lincoln hadn't even been a choice at many Southern polls! They worried that

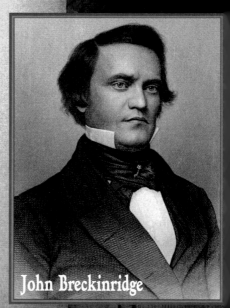

John Breckinridge

18

Lincoln would use federal power to end slavery. Some states were ready to stand against this new government. On December 20, 1860, South Carolina became the first state to secede, or withdraw, from the country.

Lincoln was a successful lawyer in Illinois before running for president.

War Begins at Fort Sumter

Mississippi, Florida, Alabama, Georgia, Louisiana, and Texas seceded soon after South Carolina. These states formed a new nation called the **Confederate** States of America, elected Jefferson Davis as their president, and even created a constitution.

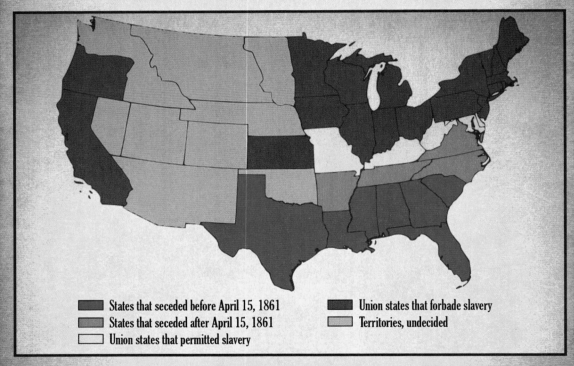

States that seceded before April 15, 1861
States that seceded after April 15, 1861
Union states that permitted slavery
Union states that forbade slavery
Territories, undecided

On April 12, 1861, the first shots of the Civil War were fired in South Carolina. Fort Sumter in the Charleston Harbor belonged to the **Union**. Jefferson Davis ordered Confederate forces to capture the fort.

Following this battle, four more states left the Union—Arkansas, North Carolina, Tennessee, and Virginia. (The western part of Virginia

This photo shows the inside of Fort Sumter the day after the Union surrendered it. An early Confederate flag is displayed.

decided to stay in the Union and became the state of West Virginia in 1863.) Four slave states stayed in the Union—Missouri, Kentucky, Maryland, and Delaware.

Both the Union and the Confederacy prepared themselves for war. From the start, the Union had more resources than the Confederacy. The Union had more factories to make weapons and more railroads to transport goods and soldiers. Also, the Union had more people—about 22 million people compared to 9 million in the Confederacy—and therefore could raise a larger army.

Major Battles of the Civil War

The Civil War took place in two main areas. In the east, most of the battles were fought between the two capital cities: the Union's Washington, D.C., and the Confederacy's Richmond, Virginia. In the west, most battles took place in Kentucky, Tennessee, and Mississippi.

First and Second Battles of Bull Run

In July 1861, Union general Irvin McDowell led his army to a creek called Bull Run near Manassas, Virginia, to attack Confederate forces. With the help of Confederate commander Thomas "Stonewall" Jackson, the Confederate army defeated the Union army. This battle was later known in the North as the First Battle of Bull Run and in the South as the First Battle of Manassas. It showed the North that the war wouldn't be won easily.

The Union and Confederacy met in Manassas again in August 1862. This time, Confederate general Robert E. Lee's army defeated Union general George McClellan's forces.

Battle of Antietam

The bloodiest day of the war was September 17, 1862. Lee led about 40,000 men onto the battlefield near Antietam Creek, Maryland, where he was met by about 90,000 Union soldiers. Lee eventually retreated, and Antietam was considered a Union victory. However, about 26,000 soldiers

The War on Film

The American Civil War was the first major conflict captured on film. Mathew Brady became famous for his photographs—often bloody and shocking—of battlefield scenes. Brady wasn't afraid to get close to the fighting and was almost captured at the First Battle of Bull Run. Brady took many photographs of Abraham Lincoln, including the one that was copied for the $5 bill. Brady took the photograph below.

had died or were wounded or missing after just 1 day of fighting. More people died during the Battle of Antietam (also known as the Battle of Sharpsburg) than during the entire American Revolution.

After the Battle of Antietam, President Abraham Lincoln (shown here at the Antietam battlefield with Union generals) issued the Emancipation Proclamation. The proclamation freed slaves in the Confederate states and allowed blacks to serve in the Union army. About 200,000 blacks joined the Union army as soldiers, cooks, scouts, and spies.

Battle of Gettysburg

In June 1863, Lee's Confederate army of 75,000 made a move to invade the North again, marching through Maryland and into Pennsylvania. Union forces of 90,000, led by General George Meade, prepared to stop him. From July 1 to July 3, the armies fought near Gettysburg. About 50,000 men were killed or wounded. Lee retreated into Virginia.

Lincoln later delivered what is known today as the Gettysburg Address, honoring the dead and promising that the Union would survive. He said that the "government of the people, by the people, for the people, shall not perish from the earth."

Shiloh and Vicksburg

West of the Appalachian Mountains, Confederate and Union forces fought for control of waterways. Union general Ulysses S. Grant's army won the Battle of Shiloh in Pittsburg Landing, Tennessee, in April 1862. In 1863, Grant organized a siege of Vicksburg, Mississippi. After 48 days, the city surrendered, giving the Union control of the Mississippi River. This cut the Confederate forces in two.

Surrender

The Confederacy grew weaker with each Union victory. Union **blockades** kept supplies from Europe from reaching Confederate states. Following a 9-month siege that ended on April 3, 1865, Petersburg, Virginia— a city that provided supplies for the Confederate capital—surrendered to Union forces. On April 9, Robert E. Lee and Ulysses S. Grant met at Appomattox Courthouse in Virginia to discuss the Confederate surrender.

On September 2, 1864, Union general William T. Sherman captured Atlanta, Georgia. His army burned and destroyed large areas of Georgia and South Carolina.

Civil War Timeline

April 12, 1861	Confederacy attacks Fort Sumter.
July 21, 1861	Confederacy wins First Battle of Bull Run.
April 7, 1862	Union wins Battle of Shiloh.
August 30, 1862	Confederacy wins Second Battle of Bull Run.
September 17, 1862	Union victory at Battle of Antietam.
July 3, 1863	Union wins at Gettysburg.
July 4, 1863	Union captures Vicksburg.
September 2, 1864	Union captures Atlanta.
April 3, 1865	Union captures Petersburg.
April 9, 1865	Confederacy surrenders at Appomattox Courthouse.

Reconstructing a Nation

The end of the American Civil War left many parts of the country, especially the South, in ruins. More than 620,000 soldiers had died. Many Southern cities had been destroyed. President Abraham Lincoln had before him the immense task of reuniting and rebuilding a nation. This period of rebuilding the South is called Reconstruction.

In January 1865, in an effort to prepare the nation for a new beginning, Congress proposed the Thirteenth **Amendment**, ending slavery in the United States. To help freed blacks build new lives, Congress created the Freedmen's Bureau to set up jobs, hospitals, and schools for blacks in the South.

From Lincoln to Johnson

Just 5 days after the meeting at Appomattox Courthouse, Lincoln was **assassinated**. Vice President Andrew Johnson became president and promised to continue Reconstruction. Johnson asked the South to make reforms before being allowed to rejoin the Union. However, under Johnson's Reconstruction plans, laws called black codes allowed blacks to be whipped by employers, sent blacks without jobs to jail, and made black children work. Many blacks found themselves in conditions similar to those before the war. Unhappy with

On April 14, 1865, Abraham Lincoln was shot by an actor and Confederate spy named John Wilkes Booth at Ford's Theatre in Washington, D.C. This picture shows Lincoln's coffin being escorted through New York City.

The Violence Continues

Around 1865, anger against blacks and Northerners resulted in the formation of the Ku Klux Klan. This group, which wrongly believed that whites were superior to blacks, was behind much of the violence toward blacks following the Civil War. Around 5,000 blacks were killed in the South in 1865 and 1866.

Johnson's policies, some members of Congress demanded that blacks be given more rights.

Congress Forces Change

In June 1866, Congress proposed the Fourteenth Amendment, which made blacks citizens. This promised them rights belonging to citizens, such as the right to own property and protection under the law. No Southern state could rejoin the Union until it **ratified** this amendment. President Johnson was unwilling to give blacks the rights of citizens. He and all states except Tennessee refused to ratify the amendment.

Despite Johnson's opposition, Congress passed several laws called the Reconstruction Acts. These laws sent military troops to govern the South while the states set up new state governments under rigid guidelines. All states had to register blacks to vote, create new state constitutions giving blacks the right to vote, and finally ratify the Fourteenth Amendment.

In 1870, the Fifteenth Amendment made it illegal for citizens to be denied the right to vote because of their race. That year, all former Confederate states were readmitted to the United States and regained their

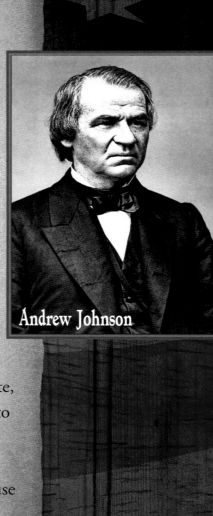

Andrew Johnson

seats in Congress. Republicans won many seats since many of the Southern Democratic leaders weren't allowed to take office. In addition, about seventeen blacks were elected to Congress.

Abraham Lincoln had chosen Andrew Johnson as his vice president because Johnson was a Southerner who wanted to keep the nation united. Johnson's Southern sympathies angered many in Congress after the war, and he was almost removed from office. In this picture, Congress narrowly votes to allow Johnson to stay in office.

After Reconstruction

By the 1870s, the Northern power over the South began to weaken. Reconstruction didn't result in a new South that recognized blacks as equals. Instead, many blacks continued to work for wealthier whites and were unable to build better lives. Separate businesses, churches, schools, and other facilities were created to keep blacks and whites apart. This separation was called segregation. New policies, such as taxes and tests, prevented blacks from voting. Poll taxes required new voters (mostly blacks) to pay money to vote. Unfair reading tests were put in place to keep blacks from voting as well.

The Civil War made the nation whole once again and ended slavery, but Americans weren't truly united. Not until the **civil rights movement** of the mid-1900s would black Americans begin to make strides in gaining the rights promised them as citizens of the United States.

Amendments to the U.S. Constitution after the Civil War

Thirteenth Amendment	Fourteenth Amendment	Fifteenth Amendment
abolished slavery in all of the United States	gave black men citizenship and all the rights and protections promised to citizens	stated that no citizen could be kept from voting because of their race

Glossary

amendment (uh-MEHND-muhnt) A change to the U.S. Constitution.

armory (AHRM-ree) A place where weapons are stored.

assassinate (uh-SAA-suh-nayt) To kill an important person, often for political reasons.

blockade (blah-KAYD) An action to stop goods and people from entering or leaving a place.

civil rights movement (SIH-vuhl RYTS MOOV-muhnt) A movement that began in the United States after World War II to win freedom and equality for all.

Confederate (kuhn-FEH-duh-reht) Describing the union of Southern states during the American Civil War.

Constitutional Convention (kahn-stuh-TOO-shuh-nuhl kuhn-VEHN-shun) A meeting of leaders from the thirteen colonies to create a body of laws for the newly formed United States of America.

electoral (ee-lehk-TOHR-uhl) Having to do with the formal body elected by voters to choose the president and vice president of the United States.

Louisiana Territory (loo-ee-zee-AA-nuh TEHR-uh-tohr-ee) A large piece of land in North America sold by France to the United States in 1803. It stretched from the Rocky Mountains in the west to the Mississippi River in the east.

Mason-Dixon Line (MAY-suhn—DIHK-suhn LYN) The boundary between Pennsylvania and Maryland, formerly separating the free states of the North from the slave states of the South. It was mapped between 1763 and 1767 by Charles Mason and Jeremiah Dixon.

popular sovereignty (PAH-pyuh-luhr SAH-vruhn-tee) The political belief that power should be placed in the hands of the public to decide an issue.

ratify (RA-tuh-fy) To approve or to agree to something in an official way.

Union (YOON-yuhn) The Northern states that stayed loyal to the national government during the Civil War.

Index